THE UKRAINE INVASION:

How Vladimir Putin built His career on waging War

ALEXANDER JACKSON

Alexander Jackson

INTRODUCTION

Vladimir Putin has undoubtedly brought oppositions in the past down to their knees in fear and goes down to be one of the Most powerful forces to reckon with in this present dispensation.

CHAPTER ONE

EARLY LIFE

Vladimir Vladimirovich Putin was brought into the world on 7 October 1952 in Leningrad, Russian SFSR, Soviet Association (presently Holy person Petersburg, Russia), Spiridon Putin, Vladimir Putin's granddad, was a singular cook to Vladimir Lenin and Joseph Stalin. First experience with the world was gone before by the passing's of two kin, Viktor and Albert, who both were brought into the world during the 1930s. Albert kicked the pail in start and Viktor passed on from diphtheria during the Assault of Leningrad by Nazi Germany's powers in All-inclusive Clash II.[22]

Putin's mom was an assembly line laborer and his dad was a recruit in the Soviet Naval force, serving in the submarine armada in the mid-1930s. From the get-go in The Second Great War, his dad served in the obliteration unit of the NKVD. Later, he was moved to the ordinary armed force and was seriously injured in 1942. Putin's maternal grandma was dispensed with by the German occupiers of Tver area in 1941, and his maternal uncles vanished on the Eastern Front during Universal Conflict II.

On 1 September 1960, Putin began at School No. 193 at Baskov Path, close to his home. He was one of a couple in the class of around 45 understudies who were not yet individuals from the Youthful Trailblazer association. At age 12, he started to rehearse sambo and judo. In his extra energy he delighted in perusing on Marx, Engels and Lenin. Putin concentrated on German at Holy person Petersburg Secondary School and communicates in German.

Putin concentrated on regulation at the Leningrad State College which is presently named Holy person Petersburg State College in 1970 and graduated in 1975. His proposition was on The Most Preferred Country Exchanging Rule Worldwide Law. While there, he was expected to join the Socialist Coalition of the Soviet Association and stayed a part until it stopped to exist (it was prohibited in August 1991). Putin met Anatoly Sobchak, an associate teacher who showed business law, and later turned into the co-creator of the Russian constitution and of the defilement plans aggrieved in France. Putin would be persuasive in Sobchak's profession in Holy person Petersburg and Sobchak would be persuasive in Putin's profession in Moscow.

Putin concentrated on regulation at Leningrad State College, where his mentor was Anatoly Sobchak, later one of the main change government officials of the perestroika time frame. Putin served 15 years as an unfamiliar insight official for the KGB (Panel for State

Security), remembering six years for Dresden, East Germany.

In 1990 he resigned from dynamic KGB administration with the position of lieutenant colonel and got back to Russia to become prorector of Leningrad State College with obligation regarding the foundations outside relations. He promptly won Sobchak's assurance and became known for his ability to complete things; by 1994 he had rose to the post of first delegate city hall leader.

In 1996 Putin moved to Moscow, where he joined the official staff as appointee to Pavel Borodin, the Kremlin's main overseer. Putin developed near individual Leningrader Anatoly Chubais and climbed in authoritative positions. In July 1998 Pres. Boris Yeltsin made Putin overseer of the Government Security Administration (FSB; the KGB's homegrown replacement), and presently he became secretary of the persuasive Security Committee. Yeltsin, who was looking for a main successor to accept his mantle, designated Putin state leader in 1999.

In spite of the fact that he was essentially obscure, Putin's public-endorsement appraisals took off when he sent off an efficient military activity against secessionist rebels in Chechnya. Wearied by long periods of Yeltsin's inconsistent conduct, the Russian public liked Putin's coolness and conclusiveness under tension. Putin's help for another constituent coalition, Solidarity, guaranteed its achievement in the December parliamentary races.

CHAPTER TWO

Political Life of Putin

1. First and second terms as leader of Russia

On December 31, 1999, Yeltsin out of the blue reported his acquiescence and named Putin acting president. Promising to modify a debilitated Russia, the somber and saved Putin handily won the Walk 2000 races with around 53% of the vote. As president, he looked to end debasement and make a firmly directed market economy.

Putin immediately reasserted command over Russia's 89 locales and republics, separating them into seven new government regions, each headed by an agent named by the president. He likewise eliminated the right of territorial lead representatives to sit in the League Chamber, the upper place of the Russian parliament. Putin moved to diminish the force of Russia's disliked lenders and media magnates the supposed "oligarchs"- by shutting a few news sources and sending off criminal procedures against various driving figures. He confronted a tough spot in Chechnya, especially from rebels who arranged fear monger assaults in Moscow and guerilla assaults on Russian soldiers from the district's mountains;

in 2002 Putin announced the tactical mission over, yet setbacks stayed high.

Putin unequivocally had a problem with U.S. Pres. George W. Shrubbery's choice in 2001 to leave the 1972 Ballistic missile destroying Rocket Settlement. Because of the September 11 assaults on the US in 2001, he vowed Russia's help and collaboration in the U.S.- drove crusade against psychological militants and their partners, offering the utilization of Russia's airspace for philanthropic conveyances and help in search-and-salvage activities. By the by, Putin joined German Chancellor Gerhard Schröder and French Pres. Jacques Chirac in 2002-03 to go against U.S. furthermore English intends to involve power to expel Saddam Hussein's administration in Iraq.

Regulating an economy that appreciated development after a drawn out downturn during the 1990s, Putin was handily reappointed in Walk 2004. In parliamentary races in December 2007, Putin's party, Joined Russia, won a staggering larger part of seats. However the reasonableness of the decisions was addressed by worldwide onlookers and by the Socialist Coalition of the Russian Alliance, the outcomes regardless insisted Putin's power. With a protected arrangement driving Putin to venture down in 2008, he picked Dmitry Medvedev as his replacement.

2. Putin as state head

Not long after Medvedev won the Walk 2008 official political race by a surprising margin, Putin reported that he had acknowledged the place of executive of the Assembled Russia party. Affirming far reaching assumptions, Medvedev assigned Putin as the nation's head of the state not long after getting to work on May 7, 2008. Russia's parliament affirmed the arrangement the next day. Despite the fact that Medvedev developed more confident as his term advanced, Putin was as yet viewed as the fundamental power inside the Kremlin.

While some estimated that Medvedev could run briefly term, he reported in September 2011 that he and Putin would-forthcoming an Assembled Russia triumph at the surveys exchange positions. Broad abnormalities in parliamentary decisions in December 2011 set off an influx of famous dissent, and Putin confronted a shockingly solid resistance development in the official race. On Walk 4, 2012, in any case, Putin was chosen for a third term as Russia's leader. Ahead of his initiation, Putin surrendered as Joined Russia administrator, giving control of the party to Medvedev. He was initiated as president on May 7, 2012, and one of his first follow upon accepting office was to designate Medvedev to fill in as top state leader.

3. The third official term of Vladimir Putin

Putin's first year back in office as president was described as a generally fruitful work to smother the dissent development. Resistance pioneers were imprisoned, and nongovernmental associations that got financing from abroad were named as "unfamiliar specialists." Pressures with the US erupted in June 2013, when U.S. Public safety Office (NSA) worker for hire Edward Snowden looked for asylum in Russia in the wake of uncovering the presence of various mystery NSA programs. Snowden was permitted to stay in Russia relying on the prerequisite that, in the expressions of Putin, he quit "carrying damage to our American accomplices." After synthetic weapons assaults outside Damascus in August 2013, the U.S. put forth the defense for military intercession in the Syrian Common Conflict. In a publication distributed in The New York Times, Putin encouraged limitation, and the U.S. what's more Russian authorities expedited an arrangement by which Syria's substance weapons supply would be obliterated. Putin honored the twentieth commemoration of the reception of the post-Soviet constitution in December 2013 by requesting the arrival of nearly 25,000 people from Russian jails. In a different move, he conceded an absolution to Mikhail Khodorkovsky, the previous top of Yuko's oil aggregate who had been detained for over 10 years on charges that numerous external Russia asserted were politically inspired.

4. The Ukraine struggle and Syrian intercession

In February 2014, when the public authority of Ukrainian Pres. Viktor Yanukovych was ousted following quite a while of supported fights, Yanukovych escaped to Russia. Declining to perceive the broken government in Kyiv as authentic, Putin mentioned parliamentary endorsement to dispatch troops to Ukraine to protect Russian interests. By early Walk 2014 Russian soldiers favorable to Russian paramilitary gatherings had actually assumed responsibility for Crimea, a Ukrainian independent republic whose populace was prevalently ethnic Russian. In a famous mandate hung on Walk 16, occupants of Crimea cast a ballot to join Russia, and Western states presented a progression of movement boycotts and resource freezes against individuals from Putin's internal circle. On Walk 18 Putin, expressing that Crimea had forever been essential for Russia, marked a settlement consolidating the promontory into the Russian Organization. Over the resulting days even a greater amount of Putin's political partners were designated with monetary approvals by the U.S. also the EU. After endorsement of the deal by the two places of the Russian parliament, on Walk 21 Putin marked a regulation that formalized the Russian addition of Crimea.

In April 2014, gatherings of unidentified shooters furnished with Russian hardware held onto government structures all through southeastern Ukraine, igniting an equipped clash with the public authority in Kyiv. Putin alluded to the district as Novorossiya ("New Russia"), summoning claims from the magnificent period, and, albeit all signs highlighted direct Russian inclusion in the rebellion, Putin relentlessly denied contributing to the battling. On July 17, 2014, Malaysia Carriers flight MH17, conveying 298 individuals, crashed in eastern Ukraine, and overpowering proof demonstrated that it had been shot somewhere near a Russian-made surface-to-air rocket discharged from rebel-a controlled area. Western nations answered by fixing the assents system, and those actions joined with diving oil costs, sent the Russian economy into a spiral. The North Atlantic Settlement Association (NATO) assessed that in excess of 1,000 Russian soldiers were effectively battling inside Ukraine when Russian and Ukrainian pioneers met for truce talks in Minsk, Belarus, on September 5. The truce eased back, however didn't stop, the viciousness, and favorable to Russian agitators went through the following while pushing back Ukrainian government powers.

On February 12, 2015, Putin met with other world innovators in Minsk to endorse a 12-point harmony plan pointed toward finishing the battling in Ukraine. Albeit battling eased back for a period, the contention got again in the spring, and by September 2015 the Assembled Countries (UN) assessed that exactly 8,000 individuals had been killed and 1.5 million had been uprooted because of the battling. On September 28, 2015, in a location before the UN General Gathering, Putin introduced his vision of Russia as a politically influential nation, equipped for projecting its impact abroad, while painting the US and NATO as dangers to worldwide security. After two days Russia turned into a functioning member in the Syrian Common Conflict, when Russian airplane struck focuses close to the urban communities of Homs and Hama. Albeit Russian safeguard authorities expressed that the air strikes were expected to target troops and matériel having a place with the Islamic State in Iraq and the Levant, the real focal point of the assaults appeared to have been on adversaries of Syrian president and Russian partner Bashar al-Assad.

5. Quieting pundits and activities in the West

On February 27, 2015, resistance pioneer Boris Nemtsov was gunned down inside sight of the Kremlin, only days after he had stood up against Russian intercession in Ukraine. Nemtsov was unquestionably the most recent Putin pundit to be killed or to pass on under dubious conditions. In January 2016 an English public request authoritatively embroiled Putin in the 2006 homicide of previous Government Security Administration (FSB; the replacement to the KGB) official Alexander Litvinenko. Litvinenko, who had stood in opposition to Russian government binds to coordinated wrongdoing both when his absconding to the Assembled Realm, was harmed with polonium-210 while savoring tea a London lodging bar. England requested the removal of the two men blamed for completing the death, however both denied contribution and one-Andrey Lugovoy had since been chosen for the Duma and appreciated parliamentary resistance from arraignment.

Aleksey Navalny, a resistance dissident who had first accomplished conspicuousness as a head of the 2011 dissent development, was over and again detained on what allies portrayed as politically propelled charges. Navalny completed second in the Moscow mayoral race in 2013, however his Advancement Party was closed out of ensuing races on procedural grounds. In the September 2016 official political decision, elector turnout was simply 47.8 percent, the most minimal since the breakdown of the Soviet Association.
 Citizen detachment was ascribed to Putin's consistent execution of supposed "oversaw majority rule government," a framework by which the fundamental constructions and strategies of a vote based system were kept up with however the result of races was generally foreordained. Putin's Unified Russia party guaranteed triumph, yet political race onlookers reported various inconsistencies, including cases of voting form stuffing and rehash casting a ballot. Navalny's party was restricted from handling any applicants as a result of its enlistment status, and Nemtsov's PARNAS gotten under 1% of the vote.

By 2016 Putin's contribution had moved the equilibrium in power in Syria, and proof arose that Russia was directing a wide-running half and half fighting effort expected to subvert the power and authenticity of Western majority rule governments. A significant number of the assaults obscured the line among cyberwarfare and cybercrime, while others reviewed the immediate Soviet interventionism of the Virus War period. Russian warrior flies regularly abused NATO airspace in the Baltic, and a couple of modern cyberattacks on the Ukrainian power matrix dove countless individuals into haziness. Ukrainian Pres. Petro Poroshenko detailed that his nation had been exposed to more than 6,000 digital interruptions north of a two-month time span, with basically every area of Ukrainian culture being designated. Poroshenko expressed that Ukrainian agents had connected the cyberwar mission to Russian security administrations. In Montenegro, where the favorable to Western government was getting ready for promotion to NATO, specialists barely turned away a plot to kill Montenegrin State head Milo Đjukanović and introduce a supportive of Russian government. Montenegrin investigators uncovered a scheme that connected patriot Serbs, favorable to Russian contenders in eastern Ukraine, and, supposedly, a couple of Russian knowledge specialists who had arranged the arranged overthrow.

In the months preceding the 2016 U.S. official political decision, a progression of prominent hacking assaults designated the Leftist alliance and its official chosen one Hillary Clinton. PC security specialists attached these assaults to Russian knowledge administrations, and in July 2016 a great many private messages were distributed by WikiLeaks. Inside the space of days the U.S. Government Department of Examination opened a test into Russian endeavors to impact the official political decision. It was subsequently uncovered that this examination was likewise analyzing potential associations between those endeavors and the mission of conservative official applicant Donald Trump. Trump kidded that Russia had delivered the hacked messages since "Putin likes me" and later welcomed Russia to "find [Clinton's] 30,000 messages that are missing." notwithstanding these articulations, Trump over and again excused the likelihood that Putin was endeavoring to influence the political decision in support of himself.

After Trump's dazzling triumph in November 2016, recharged consideration was centered around the cyberattacks and conceivable intrigue between Trump's mission group and Russia. U.S. knowledge offices reasoned that Putin had requested a multipronged mission to impact the political race and subvert confidence in American popularity based frameworks. U.S. Pres. Barack Obama forced financial approvals on Russian knowledge benefits and removed many presumed

Russian agents, however President-elect Trump kept on dismissing the finishes of U.S. insight offices. Trump got to work in January 2017 and extra examinations were opened by the U.S. Congress to look at the nature and degree of Russian interfering in the official political decision.
As far as concerns him, Putin denied the presence of any mission to impact unfamiliar races. In May 2017, notwithstanding, one more cyberattack was ascribed to Fancy Bear, the Russian government-connected bunch that had completed the hack on the Progressive alliance. France was holding the second round of its official

political race, and the finalists were moderate Emmanuel Macron and extreme right Public Front up-and-comer Marine Le Pen. Le Pen had recently gotten monetary help from a bank that had connections to the Kremlin, and she pledged to push for the finish of the assents system that had been instituted after Russia's addition of Crimea. Only hours before a media power outage on crusade related news inclusion came full circle, a gigantic store of inside correspondences named "MacronLeaks" surfaced on the Web. This work failed miserably, as Macron caught almost two times however many votes as Le Pen and became leader of France.

Putin's unfamiliar moves seemed to deliver huge profits at home, as his famous endorsement rating reliably stayed over 80% despite Russia's slow economy and endemic government defilement. Low oil costs and Western authorizations intensified an all around terrible monetary viewpoint as unfamiliar financial backers stayed hesitant to place their capital in danger in a land where individual connections to Putin were viewed as more significant than law and order. Indeed, even after Russia arose out of seven successive quarters of downturn, the two wages and shopper spending stayed stale in 2017. These and other homegrown issues appeared to do close to nothing to gouge Putin's picture; among those communicating worry for such issues in assessments of public sentiment, fault was most frequently attached to Putin's head of the state, Dmitry Medvedev.

6. Fourth official term

Salisbury novichok assault and relationship with Trump
As the Walk 2018 official political race drew closer, it
appeared to be everything except sure that Putin would
win a fourth official term by a long shot. Navalny, the
substance of the resistance, was banished from running,
and the Socialist applicant, Pavel Grudinin, confronted
unremitting analysis from the state-run media. Fourteen
days before the political race, Putin turned into the focal
point of a significant global episode when Sergei Skripal,
a previous Russian insight official who was indicted for
spying for England just to be delivered to the Assembled
Realm as a component of a detainee trade, was tracked
down oblivious with his girl in Salisbury, Britain.
Examiners affirmed that the pair had been presented to a
"novichok," a complicated nerve specialist created by the
Soviets. English authorities blamed Putin for having
requested the assault, and English State leader Theresa
May ousted almost two dozen Russian knowledge agents
who had been working in England under discretionary
cover.
The discretionary line had not subsided when Russians
went to the surveys on Walk 18, 2018. The date was, not
unintentionally, the fourth commemoration of Russia's
coercive extension of the Ukrainian independent republic
of Crimea, an occasion that undeniable a spike in Putin's
homegrown fame. True to form, Putin asserted a
staggering greater part of the vote in a political race that
free checking organization Golos described as being
overflowing with inconsistencies. Putin had wanted for a

higher turnout than in his 2012 political decision triumph, and voting form stuffing was seen in various areas. Putin's mission portrayed the outcome as an "unbelievable triumph."

On July 16, 2018, straight from the achievement of Russia's generally welcomed facilitating of the World Cup football title, Putin held a highest point meeting in Helsinki with Trump. The two had directed conversations at the Gathering of 20 (G20) culmination in Hamburg, Germany, and the Asia-Pacific Financial Collaboration gathering in Da Nang, Vietnam, in 2017, yet the experience in Finland denoted their first proper one-on-one gathering. It came toward the finish of Trump's excursion to Europe where he had unsettled relations with the US's conventional European partners. Albeit a few eyewitnesses addressed whether Trump would have the option to stand his ground in conversations with a partner as prepared and cagey as Putin, Trump said that he figured his gathering with Putin would be the "simplest" of his excursion.

After Putin kept Trump holding up by showing up later than expected, the two met alone (with just interpreters present) for nearly two hours and afterward more momentarily within the sight of counsels. In the public interview that followed, Putin indeed denied any Russian impedance in the 2016 U.S. official political race. Trump then, at that point, sent shock waves when, in light of a correspondent's inquiry, he showed that he believed Putin's forswearing more than the finishes of his own insight associations, which just days sooner had brought about the U.S. Division of Equity's incrimination of 12 Russian insight specialists for their intruding in the political race. Additionally, offered the chance to denounce intrusive Russian activities, Trump rather cast fault on the US for its stressed relationship with Russia. Trump additionally warmed to Putin's proposal to permit U.S. examiners to meet with the Russian specialists as a trade-off for Russian admittance to Americans of premium in Russian examinations asked by an American columnist assuming he had inclined toward Trump in the political decision, Putin said that he had, on account of Trump's communicated craving for better relations with Russia. Whenever examined regarding whether Russia had kompromat (compromising data) on Trump, Putin highlighted the St. Petersburg Monetary Gathering and discussed the inconceivability of acquiring compromising material on every one of the more than 500 "high-positioning, significant level" American money managers said to have gone to the meeting. He additionally said that he had been uninformed about Trump's presence in Moscow during a previous visit. Some press records of his response, nonetheless, called attention to that Putin didn't unequivocally deny having Trump-related kompromat. The Russian press trumpeted the culmination as a gigantic accomplishment for Putin. Russian Unfamiliar Clergyman Sergey Lavrov portrayed the result of the culmination as "better than super." The reaction in the US was for the most part shock, and various conservatives joined leftists in firmly denouncing Trump's presentation.

CHAPTER THREE

Ukraine invasion: how Vladimir Putin built his career on waging war

Established change and the assault on Ukraine

In spite of the fact that Russia remained something of an outcast on the worldwide stage-its competitors were banned from global contest because of a gigantic state-supported doping plan, it was suspended endlessly from the G8, and it was the objective of a pile of monetary authorizations Putin's own height was undiminished. With England attempting to finish up a leave manage the European Association, German Chancellor Angela Merkel in the nightfall of her residency as true head of Europe, and states in Poland and Hungary showing progressively tyrant rehearses, Putin confronted a West that appeared to not be able to track down its bearing. Against this scenery he bragged a vigorous extension of Russian military power, especially in the field of hypersonic weapons. Talking about the noteworthy weapons contest between the U.S. also the Soviet Association, in December 2019 Putin commented, "Today, we have what is going on that is special in present day history: they're attempting to get up to speed to us."

In January 2020 Putin declared his expectation to alter the Russian constitution in a manner that would scrap service time boundaries presidents, making ready for him to stay in office endlessly. Medvedev instantly surrendered as state leader, expressing that another administration would offer Putin "the chance to settle on the choices he really wants to make." The proposed established changes were rapidly endorsed by the Russian governing body, yet Putin booked a public mandate with regards to this issue, a move that pundits depicted as minimal more than political theater. That vote was initially planned for April, however it was delayed until July because of the Coronavirus pandemic. Obviously, the outcome was a mind-boggling certification of Putin's plan, however resistance bunches noticed that there was no autonomous checking of the political race process.

On August 20 Navalny turned out to be genuinely sick on a departure from the Siberian city of Tomsk, and tests later affirmed that he had been presented to a novichok. Navalny was traveled to Germany to recuperate, and the next month resistance competitors performed shockingly well in nearby decisions held in the space where Navalny had been crusading. The Kremlin denied inclusion in the harming, yet such protestations had become progressively unrealistic, as the assault on Navalny addressed just the latest in a long series of endeavors on the existences of Putin's faultfinders.

In late 2021 Putin requested a huge development of Russian powers along the Ukrainian line; extra units were dispatched to Belarus, apparently to take part in joint activities with the Belarusian military. Western states raised worries concerning what had all the earmarks of being an impending Russian intrusion, yet Putin rejected that he had any such plans. By February 2022 upwards of 190,000 Russian soldiers were ready to strike into Ukraine from forward bases in Russia, Russian-involved Crimea, Belarus, and the Russian-moved rebel area of Transdniestria in Moldova. What's more, land and/or water capable units were conveyed to the Dark Ocean underhandedly. On February 21 Putin perceived the freedom of oneself broadcasted individuals' republics of Donetsk and Luhansk, actually voiding the 2015 Minsk nonaggression treaty. In the early morning long periods of February 24 Putin declared the start of a "exceptional military activity," and blasts could be heard in urban areas across Ukraine. Ukrainian Pres. Volodymyr Zelensky said that his nation would shield itself, and Western pioneers denounced the unmerited assault, promising quick and extreme approvals against Russia.

counting non socialist, however the Socialist Coalition kept on ruling the framework

Ukraine intrusion: how Vladimir Putin fabricated his profession on taking up arms

The Russian president's profession is saturated with blood. Yet, the attack of Ukraine is more aggressive, and unsafe, than anything the Russian president has endeavored previously

Second Chechen conflict 1999-2000

In September 1999, a month after Putin became PM, bomb blasts at apartment complexes in Moscow and two different urban communities killed north of 300 individuals. Putin accused Chechen separatists (who denied it). He requested the air besieging of Grozny - the beginning of the subsequent Chechen conflict. Alexander Litvinenko, the ex-FSB specialist killed in London in 2006, guaranteed the FSB established the city bombs, with Putin's intrigue, to assist with presenting to him the administration. That was rationale enough for his harming. The conflict left up to 50,000 dead or missing, generally regular folks.

Intrusion of Georgia 2008

As in the Donbas today, nonconformist powers in the breakaway Georgian locales of South Ossetia and Abkhazia battled government powers in August 2008. At the point when Georgia's leader, Mikheil Saakashvili, sent troops to reestablish request, Putin conveyed Russian powers to help the separatists (which they had as of now been doing). A full-scale Russian attack of an undisputed Georgian area followed in what the future holds "implementation" activity.

Intrusion of Ukraine 2014

Again following up on the guise of safeguarding abused ethnic Russians, powers under Putin's bearing held onto control of parts of Luhansk and Donetsk oblasts in eastern Ukraine (part of the Donbas locale) in 2014. The two dissenter substances announced their freedom this month. Putin additionally attached Crimea. An expected 14,000 individuals have passed on in battling paving the way to the current struggle.

Barack Obama's inability to mediate in Syria's affable conflict after a compound assault in Ghouta in 2013, which had penetrated the US president's "red line", left an opening for Putin. Expectation on taking advantage of American shortcoming, supporting his partner, Syria's leader, Bashar åal-Assad, and reinforcing Russia's essential situation in the Center East, Putin sent planes and exceptional powers to Syria in 2015. They are still there. Russia presently has an extremely durable maritime base on the Mediterranean, at Tartus.

CHAPTER FOUR

CONCLUSION

In what currently resembles a dress practice for the Ukraine attack, Putin sent troops to Kazakhstan, one more previous Soviet republic, in January. Yet rather than bring down the officeholder system, their central goal was to assist the country's rulers with smothering supportive of a majority rule government fights started by financial difficulty and defilement. In recognizable style, Putin again portrayed the soldiers as "peacekeepers". By all accounts, the activity was moderately bloodless.